Rich

CRAIG RAINE

Rich

ff

faber and faber

LONDON · BOSTON

First published in 1984
by Faber and Faber Limited
3 Queen Square London WC1N 3AU

Typeset by Wilmaset Birkenhead
Printed in Great Britain by
Whitstable Litho Ltd Whitstable Kent
All rights reserved

British Library Cataloguing in Publication Data

Raine, Craig
Rich.
I. Title
821'.914   PR6068.A313

ISBN 0–571–13215–4
ISBN 0–571–13308–8 (Pbk)

Dios es en realidad nada más que otro artista. Inventó la jirafa, el elefante, y el gato. No tiene ningún verdadero estilo. Sólo sigue experimentando con otras cosas.

Picasso

Contents

Acknowledgements   *page* 11

Part I: Rich

Rich   15
In Modern Dress   18
Code Napoléon   21
City Gent   23
Pornography   25
Arsehole   26
Wulf and Eadwacer   27
An Attempt at Jealousy   28
Gauguin   30
Placebo   31
Inca   34
A Free Translation   36
Words on the Page   39

Part II: A Silver Plate   43

Part III: Poor

A Walk in the Country   67
The Widower   70
Plain Song   74
Again   76
Baize Doors   80
The Season in Scarborough 1923   82
Circus   85
The Sylko Bandit   88
A Hungry Fighter   92

The Gift   95
The Man Who Invented Pain   98
Purge   102
The Grey Boy   105
The First Lesson   108

Acknowledgements

The *Age Monthly Review, Aldeburgh Festival Catalogue*, the *Antioch Review, Country Life, Critical Quarterly, Grand Street, Helix*, the *Honest Ulsterman, In Touch*, the *Kenyon Review*, the *London Review of Books*, the *New Statesman, Nieuw Vlaams Tijdschrift, NRC Handelsblad*, the *Observer, Partisan Review*, the *Penguin Book of Contemporary British Poetry*, the *Poetry Book Society Supplement*, Radio 3, the *Sewanee Review*, the *South Bank Show*, and *The Times Literary Supplement*.

In 1981, six of these poems were published as a pamphlet, *A Free Translation*, by the Salamander Press, Edinburgh. 'Baize Doors' was published in the *American Scholar*. 'In Modern Dress' first appeared in *Poems for Shakespeare 9*, edited by Dannie Abse. 'Words on the Page' was a limited edition poster poem printed by Sunderland Polytechnic, and 'Pornography' was printed by the Starwheel Press with an illustrative etching. Ten of the love poems were set to music by Nigel Osborne and performed on the South Bank in 1985. 'A Silver Plate' is a revised and expanded version of a lecture given to the Open University in the summer of 1982. 'Rich', 'In Modern Dress', 'Circus' and 'The Man Who Invented Pain' can be heard on the Faber Poetry Cassette *Thom Gunn and Craig Raine*.

As most readers will realize, I have freely adapted to my own purposes work by Dante, Marina Tsvetayeva, Rimbaud, the anonymous Anglo-Saxon poet of 'Wulf and Eadwacer' and Ford Madox Ford. My debt to these authors is very general: they were inspirations, not detailed models. I have borrowed an expression from Timothy Mo's fine novel *Sour Sweet* – to 'wipe someone's face', meaning to kill someone – a deceptive euphemism that deserves wider currency. 'The Widower' and 'The Gift' owe everything to George Katkov and his late wife, Elisabeth – Stary and Cooee to their friends.

Part I

Rich

What did that mean, to kiss? You put your face up like that to say good night and then his mother put her face down. That was to kiss. His mother put her lips on his cheek; her lips were soft and they wetted his cheek; and they made a tiny little noise: kiss. Why did people do that with their two faces?

James Joyce, *A Portrait of the Artist as a Young Man*

Rich

She owns that thoroughbred
smouldering under his blanket,
those binoculars *en croûte*
kept warm by her breasts,

and these are her eggshells
cracked on the kitchen table
like an umpire's snail
of cricketers' caps.

I woo her with words,
I number her many possessions:
seven rings by the soap,
two on top of the Steinway,

her grinning grand
with its dangerous fin.
And the boy belongs to her
who drives his toast

round a difficult bend
with multiplied lips,
or settles to sleep
by sipping his thumb.

She cannot ever know
the extent of her riches,
the mother of this naked girl
who stretches sideways,

a tired toxophilite
bending her invisible bow.
Custodian, I guard
and garner up each treasure.

She is the giver of gifts
without number or name:
this flock of crumbs
on her tablecloth,

the goldfish mouthing
its mantra, the pungency
of pencil sharpenings,
perfume by Paco Rabanne.

Her cattle are children,
each with a streaming cold,
and this is her bull
drooling over his dummy,

his angular buttocks
crusted with cradle cap.
She gives them grass.
They drink from her bath,

or gravitate towards the pond,
her snooker table, torn,
where only one player
attends to a solitary red.

And there, beyond the books
on the windowsill, her floods,
transforming the world
like the eye in love.

I am the steward
of her untold wealth,
keeper of the dictionary,
treasurer of valuables,

accountant and teller,
and I woo her with words
against the day of divorce.
Mistress of death and of birth,

she owns the trout
tortured with asthma
and this field in spring,
threadbare with green.

In Modern Dress

A pair of blackbirds
warring in the roses,
one or two poppies

losing their heads,
the trampled lawn
a battlefield of dolls.

Branch by pruned branch,
a child has climbed
the family tree

to queen it over us:
we groundlings search
the flowering cherry

till we find her face,
its pale prerogative
to rule our hearts.

Sir Walter Raleigh
trails his comforter
about the muddy garden,

a full-length Hilliard
in miniature hose
and padded pants.

How rakishly upturned
his fine moustache
of oxtail soup,

foreshadowing, perhaps,
some future time
of altered favour,

stuck in the high chair
like a pillory, features
pelted with food.

So many expeditions
to learn the history
of this little world:

I watch him grub
in the vegetable patch
and ponder the potato

in its natural state
for the very first time,
or found a settlement

of leaves and sticks,
cleverly protected
by a circle of stones.

But where on earth
did he manage to find
that cigarette end?

Rain and wind.
The day disintegrates.
I observe the lengthy

inquisition of a worm
then go indoors to face
a scattered armada

19

of picture hooks
on the dining room floor,
the remains of a ruff

on my glass of beer,
Sylvia Plath's *Ariel*
drowned in the bath.

Washing hair, I kneel
to supervise a second rinse
and act the courtier:

tiny seed pearls,
tingling into sight,
confer a kind of majesty.

And I am author
of this toga'd tribune
on my aproned lap,

who plays his part
to an audience of two,
repeating my words.

Code Napoléon

Old Sammler with his screwy visions! He saw the
increasing triumph of Enlightenment – Liberty,
Fraternity, Equality, Adultery!
Saul Bellow: *Mr Sammler's Planet*

A tricolour articulates,
unable to escape
its repertoire of vehemence

and pigeons body forth
the granite dizziness
of a duke on his plinth,

before settling like scree.
In the fishmarket,
plunder from Spain:

kilos of castanets
and one child, executing
his angry flamenco.

A little corpulent,
I am Buonaparte
with a hand on my wallet,

watching this escapologist
illustrate Rousseau
in the Place Beaubourg,

while I daydream again
the floor-length cream
of your dressing gown.

Sift in the navel,
tied at the waist,
lisping silk from Samarkand.

How the bow held its breath,
seeking to swoon,
absolved of itself . . .

But I thought of a barrister
addressing a brief,
twitching the tape undone.

City Gent

On my desk, a set of labels
or a synopsis of leeks,
blanched by the sun
and trailing their roots

like a watering can.
Beyond and below,
diminished by distance,
a taxi shivers at the lights:

a shining moorhen
with an orange nodule
set over the beak,
taking a passenger

under its wing.
I turn away, confront
the cuckold hatstand
at bay in the corner,

and eavesdrop (bless you!)
on a hay-fever of brakes.
My *Caran d'Ache* are sharp
as the tips of an iris

and the four-tier file
is spotted with rust:
a study of plaice
by a Japanese master,

ochres exquisitely bled.
Instead of office work,
I fish for complements
and sport a pencil

behind each ear,
a bit of a devil,
or trap the telephone
awkwardly under my chin

like Richard Crookback,
crying, A horse! A horse!
My kingdom for a horse!
but only to myself,

ironically: the tube
is semi-stiff with stallion whangs,
the chairman's Mercedes
has windscreen wipers

like a bird's broken tongue,
and I am perfectly happy
to see your head, quick
round the door like a dryad,

as I pretend to be Ovid
in exile, composing *Tristia*
and sad for the shining,
the missed, the muscular beach.

Pornography

Noi leggevamo un giorno per diletto . . .

They were already naked on the bed.
His hands were shaking, so,
as if he took an oath

and then the Aretine was open
like a two-way mirror:
the shining boletus

was solid with blood,
labia on a snail were black,
mistletoe was tart with sperm.

The erotic image held her.
She felt excitement
like a dying salmon in his lap

and turned her face away
towards her lover's face.
Their lips met in a kiss

that was dry with desire,
like an artist's starved brush
extending its range

to paint the guilty pictures
in their guiltless heads.
That day, we read no more.

Arsehole

It is shy as a gathered eyelet
neatly worked in shrinking violet;
it is the dilating iris, tucked
away, a tightening throb when fucked.

It is a soiled and puckered hem,
the golden treasury's privy purse.
With all the colours of a bruise,
it is the fleck of blood in albumen.

I dreamed your body was an instrument
and this was the worn mouthpiece
to which my breathing lips were bent.

Each note pleaded to love a little longer,
longer, as though it was dying of hunger.
I fed that famished mouth my ambergris.

Wulf and Eadwacer

Nothing was said. Ever. Just stares.
They would have wiped his face,
as it is wiped now in any case:
the shape of his lips, his tongue

and the touch of it, are wrong.
Now I remember only the hairs
on the back of his slim hands,
holding mine at the edge of our lands

when we said that goodbye.
So vivid they seemed. So black.
I could not look him in the eyes.
When he promised to come back

for me, after winter, in the dark,
I knew that I could wait forever,
ill with every dog's bark,
each splash from the river.

I do not want him to return now.
I could never explain how
the other one I do not love
came every day and would not move.

A soldier. Nothing was said.
He watched me and the unmade bed,
his fist frigging the dice all day.
I missed you is so easy to say.

An Attempt at Jealousy

So how is life with your new bloke?
Simpler, I bet. Just one stroke
of his quivering oar and the skin
of the Thames goes into a spin,

eh? How is life with an oarsman? Better?
More in–out? Athletic? Wetter?
When you hear the moan of the rowlocks,
do you urge him on like a cox?

Tell me, is he bright enough to find
that memo-pad you call a mind?
Or has he contrived to bring you out –
given you an in-tray and an out?

How did I ever fall for a paper-clip?
How could I ever listen to office gossip
even in bed and find it so intelligent?
Was it straight biological bent?

I suppose you go jogging together?
Tackle the Ridgeway in nasty weather?
Face force 5 gales and chat about prep
or how you bested that Birmingham rep?

He must be mad with excitement.
So must you. What an incitement
to lust all those press-ups must be.
Or is it just the same? PE?

Tell me, I'm curious. Is it fun
being in love with just anyone?
How do you remember his face
if you meet in a public place?

Perhaps you know him by his shoes?
Or do you sometimes choose
another pinstriped clone
by accident and drag that home

instead? From what you say,
he's perfect. For a Chekhov play.
Tall and dark and brightly dim,
Kulygin's part was made for him.

Imagine your life with a 'beak'.
Week after week after week
like homework or detention;
all that standing to attention

whenever his colleagues drop in
for a spot of what's-your-toxin.
Speech Day, matron, tuck-shop, Christ,
you'll find school fees are over-priced

and leave, but not come back to me.
You've done your bit for poetry.
Words, or deeds? You'll stick to youth.
I'm a stickler for the truth –

which makes me wonder what it was
I loved you for. Tell me, because
now I feel nothing – except regret.
What is it, love, I need to forget?

Gauguin

They going upstair
take longtime lookit shedownstair.

They going upstair
so hedownstair go plenty upstair.

He stickyout number2tongue,
because he magnetized to she.

Which she hide in shesecrets,
because she magnetized to he.

They making the mirror, shhh,
numberonetongues completely tied.

Shebody making the horse
and the frog, the safe shescissor,

the squat on sheback, showing
shekipper tenminute longtime,

till he cry like a candle
and heflame blow out.

Handmake Kodak man, come back,
my secrets are sorry with oil.

Placebo

And here are the dead,
raising a napkin, reaching
for salt, or a little more
non-vintage Chablis.

Cracked willow pattern
contains the lobster,
scraping its claws
like someone crouched

to keep wicket at Lord's.
Nothing can interrupt.
I want them to turn
with all their lost words.

A resurrection of silver
shines in the walnut canteen.
A cucumber sandwich
is curling its lip.

The placebo cures regret.
It brings a portrait
done by Picasso. You see?
The eyes swim together,

the nostrils fluctuate,
and I know we are close.
There is breath on my beard.
Could I forget so much?

I recognize these breasts
by their weight, this arsehole
by its blind perfection.
Nothing is censored,

not a chicken pox scar,
not the harelip glistening
between her legs.
Iron filings shine

in her shaven armpits.
This blood on my hands
is a side effect: I try
instead to concentrate

on her concentration,
each feverish tremor,
the fading linea nigra
left by her tights,

the cold touch of rings
on her shaking left hand.
I note the serious symptoms.
Suddenly like Matisse

in a three-piece suit
and consultant's white coat,
I take infinite pains
to keep this model alive.

But the day will come
with morning sickness,
when flowers fidget
in the dirty garden

and lavatories throw up,
when I am widower,
wanking and weeping
for all that is lost.

I will burgle drawers
in the children's room,
tie neat moustaches
on two pairs of shoes,

bury her head in my books.
Afternoons, I convalesce,
play patience, match-make
a court of Siamese twins.

Later, I take off my watch
to let it spread its wings.
The children are breathing
and here are the dead.

Inca

The Inca Empire, centred on Cuzco, Peru, reached its greatest extent in the 15th c., from Ecuador to N. Chile. Despite the absence of the wheel and a system of writing, it achieved a high level of civilization . . .

Longman's English Larousse

Inca. Now there is only this.
Since the past is past,
the future is fiction:
a garden with walls
where I stand in another life,

the luminous deckchair
poised like a cricket
in stifling moonlight.
The sun dial registers shadow,
made faint by the house lights.

And the swans display
their dripping beaks for us,
but your lips are parted:
to kiss, or to speak.
I cannot tell. Inca.

Now, there is only this:
the lawn sprinkler's dervish,
a rosewood metronome
whose key was lost,
and will never be found.

Inca. We will watch the pigeons
pass from grey to white,
suddenly twitched,
like a Venetian blind
in the other bedroom.

There, where the child sleeps. Inca.
I am lost in thought,
trying to write.
The water butt juggles
with raindrops. Inca.

Tears come to your eyes
as you read the blank paper
for what it can tell you.
Now, there is only this:
the long, unwritten poem

which almost celebrates
a daughter's parsnip heels
and her pale, perfect nipples
like scars left by leaves.
Inca. How her nightdress rides up.

How she comes, a serious face,
from every corner of the garden,
cupping a secret
she wants me to see,
as if she had somehow

invented the wheel. O Inca.

A Free Translation

for Norma Kitson

Seeing the pagoda
of dirty dinner plates,
I observe my hands

under the kitchen tap
as if they belonged
to Marco Polo:

glib with soap,
they speak of details
from a pillow book,

the fifty-seven ways
in which the Yin
receives the Yang.

Rinsed and purified,
they flick off drops
like a court magician

whose stretching fingers
seek to hypnotize
the helpless house . . .

This single bullrush
is the silent firework
I have invented

to amuse the children.
Slow sideboard sparkler,
we watch its wadding

softly fray.
Your skein of wool
sleeps on the sofa,

a geisha girl
with skewered hair,
too tired to think

of loosening ends,
or fret forever
for her Samurai,

whose shrunken ghost
attacks the window pane –
still waspish

in his crisp corselet
of black and gold
hammered out by Domaru.

In coolie hats,
the peasant dustbins
hoard their scraps,

careless of the warrior class . . .
It is late, late:
we have squeezed

a fluent ideogram
of cleansing cream
across the baby's bottom.

It is time to eat
the rack of pork
which curves and sizzles

like a permanent wave
by Hokusai,
time to bend

to a bowl of rice,
time to watch
your eyes become

Chinese with laughter
when I say that
orientals eat with stilts.

Words on the Page

In the bare bedroom,
with the wire handle
hung like a chinstrap,

one white billy can
holds in its head
a vision of flowers

and fragile grasses
unplaiting their seed.
Incunabula,

still sharply printed
by your underwear,
you pluck two earrings,

one by one, like fruit,
and bring yourself to bed
with tingling lobes.

Part II

A Silver Plate

All the influences were lined up waiting for me. I was born, and there they were to form me, which is why I tell you more of them than of myself.

Saul Bellow, *The Adventures of Augie March*

I was born in 1944. In the thirties, my father had been a painter and decorator, plumber, electrician, publican and boxer, but when I was growing up, he was a Spiritualist and a faith healer, talking about his negro spirit-guide, Massa, and explaining how he knew when people were cured because he felt burning coals in the palms of his hands. Inspiration ran in the family. My father would explain how he dreamed about the ill and how, for instance, in the case of Bobby Bowen's hand, paralysed after a pit accident, he'd worked on the fingers for days without success until, in a dream, the answer had come. Asleep, he'd felt a terrible pain in his upper arm. After that, he ignored the hand and massaged Bobby's arm until he felt the sensation of burning coals. The fingers, however, still didn't function and the hospital was going to amputate on the following Wednesday. 'You're better,' my father said. The miner left the house gloomily but returned in half an hour with the fingers working. He had gone to the lavatory and pressed the flush absent-mindedly with the damaged hand. There was a click and the fingers worked.

Sometimes my father would explain how you should never massage to the heart. Instead you should massage to the body's natural outlets – the tips of the fingers, the ends of the toes and the base of the spine. My mother, a devout Catholic, would listen neutrally, though she disliked the Spiritualist chapel. They had no Latin, no aspergil, no ritual. She told me once that Spiritualists ate sweets during the service. My brother and I were brought up in the Catholic faith. My father had become a Spiritualist almost by accident. Someone – he can't remember who – had dared him to attend a service. He'd

43

gone and been impressed with what he'd been told by the visiting medium, though he wasn't convinced. And the medium knew it. He told my father that he could see my father's guide and that proof was possible: all my father had to do was relax on a bed, say the Lord's Prayer, then call out the name Massa.

My father's account of this experiment is full of statistics. He is five foot four inches tall, the double bed was six foot long. He called out, 'Massa,' and was taken over – whuff! – by an enormous physical presence. When it was over, the top of his head ached where it had been crammed up against the headboard and there were red marks just below his knees where his legs had gone over the footboard. 'That made me six foot seven inches tall.'

He made no money from his cures. We were poor and the people who came were poor. The medium had also told him that he had a gift, but he didn't discover it until my older brother, just after the war, contracted polio and was discharged from hospital with a paralysed arm and leg. My father threw his calipers away and went to Charlie Hancock the chemist, who made him up a bottle of oil from an old family recipe. Today, my brother is a perfect physical specimen, except that he has to turn his hand slightly to get it out of his pocket.

Apart from the odd patient, my father did nothing. He lived on a war pension, having been invalided out of the RAF with epilepsy – the result, we think, of an explosion in a munitions factory. He was a bomb armourer in some undisclosed, remote part of Scotland. But no one knows the exact details: when the accident happened, the War Office was secretive and my father remembers nothing except waking up in hospital and the five major brain operations that followed to remove bits of shrapnel from his triple-fractured skull. There are, however, clues of a sort. My father often talks in his sleep and sometimes he speaks fluently in a foreign language. We used to think it must be Polish because two other patients in adjacent beds were Poles. We assumed he picked it up subconsciously. But my wife, who is a Russian speaker, has witnessed this particular drama and says it isn't a Slav language. When he is speaking in tongues, the pattern is always the same. In the recurrent nightmare, my father becomes angry and denounces someone. He spits with contempt and then begins to whimper suddenly and pick things off his body with a disgusted expression on his face. We think these must be bits of flesh. It is a theory, though, which doesn't account for the language. That remains a mystery like so much else.

The operations were part of my childhood. My father liked talking about them. In brain surgery then, there was only a local anaesthetic and the patient was semiconscious. My father remembers the whirr and bite of the saw that took off the top of his skull. They removed part of his brain and inserted a silver plate. As a child, I thought about this a good deal and my father would often invite me to feel the holes in his head – taking my fingers in his hand and guiding them to the slight depressions under his vaselined hair. It was like feeling the soft dints at the top of a coconut. Occasionally, he would produce from these holes a tiny sliver of bloody bone. The biggish ones were kept for the doctors at Dunstan Hill Hospital, just outside Newcastle, where they monitored his progress and adjusted his drugs. The smaller bits we'd look at for a time and then he'd throw them on the fire. Once a year, he would go into hospital for a month-long check-up. During this time, the rest of the family might take a holiday – staying in the attic of Uncle Jim's boarding house at Morecambe Bay, where my mother helped with the cooking and serving, or borrowing Auntie Mary's caravan for a week at Saltburn.

On average, we'd visit my father twice: the bus ride was long and expensive. I'd climb into my father's bed with my shoes and raincoat on to eat a jar of malt extract that had been carefully saved.

He was a good father and, since he was unemployed, I saw a lot of him. He was and is a brilliant raconteur, with a large repertoire of brutal boxing stories, in which he is always the hero. He turned professional when he was sixteen and fought for the featherweight title of Great Britain, a bout he lost to Micky McGuire. According to him, he lost on a foul punch. He knocked down McGuire for a count of nine and on the break from the subsequent clinch McGuire hit him in the adam's apple. You weren't allowed to punch on the break. For the rest of the round, my father took such a pasting that his father, who was in his corner, threw the towel in. My mother says he didn't train enough because he was going out with a girl called Ticky Hinton. This was before my parents were married, so I think my mother is guessing. Shortly after this fight, my father was reinstated amateur and, as an amateur, he fought for England against Germany in 1937 at the Albert Hall, beating Otto Kastner, the Olympic champion and Golden Gloves winner. No, that's wrong: Kastner had beaten the Golden Gloves winner. Many of his boxing stories take place in less glamorous circumstances – fairground boxing booths, for instance. Nearly all of them use a formulaic phrase: 'I dug him downstairs and his belly rolled over to there.' My father points to half-way up his forearm. I know most of his stories by heart. When he tells them now, I listen for variants and improvements. They are finished works of art, full of mimicry and telling gesture. 'And I marked him *there* and *there* and *there*': his big index finger presses hard against your nose, your eye, your mouth. Perhaps because his stories are so worked and practised, I find them useless

46

as raw material. If they were raw material once, they aren't any longer. My mother's spontaneous memories are more amenable: she can remember the trivial in a way I find exciting: 'The ginger-haired Dent twins running about naked in the back-alley to get dry after their bath.'

My father was a genius at storytelling. As a very small child, I'd sit and listen while he read me the comic. I once told my brother the comic after my father had read it to me earlier. My elder brother was amazed. 'Our Craig can *read*.' I couldn't. But the pictures triggered off my father's remembered commentary. I recall how he used to tell the story of the three pigs: when the wolf ate the pigs who'd built their houses of straw and twigs, my father would gather me up and rub his bristly face against mine, saying, 'Gnaggle, gnaggle, gnaggle.' Prodigal mimesis from which I've learned.

I also admired the way he could peel an apple with the skin in one piece, coiled like a spring. That seemed artistic, too. However, my mother stopped buying fruit. It was a status symbol and my father, she complained, just ate it. We were always short of money. For a time, my parents did a Sunday morning paper round as a way of supplementing my father's small pension. They got up at five, leaving us alone but asleep, and returned by eight o'clock. Finally, though, they quarrelled with the newsagent – my grandfather – and my mother took in sewing instead, alterations sent by an aunt who ran a dress shop, Rymer's. Another source of income was concert parties: my father was part of a double act with his brother, Charlie; Charlie was the gent in white tie and tails, my father played the village idiot in a ginger wig with most of his teeth blacked out. My father slept with an indelible pencil and paper by his bed because gags often came to him in his sleep and he'd wake up laughing. Sometimes he and Charlie would spend a

Saturday afternoon playing a George Formby record again and again until they'd got all the words of 'I'm Leaning on a Lamppost' or 'Chinese Laundry Blues'. I was allowed to play with the greasepaints and I can still smell that ginger wig with its clammy net under the coarse hair.

The concert parties eventually stopped, too. There was a quarrel about how much my father was paid in relation to Harold Swan. Harold got more because he sang *and* told jokes, but my mother maintained that he didn't sing well and that his jokes were blue. In any case, my father was obviously a bit of an embarrassment to his brother: Harold Swan pressed home the point that my father might have a fit during a performance. It was true enough and my mother's only response was to criticize the Swans for getting married and having no children because they were selfish. If it sounds quarrelsome, it was. My mother took offence quickly and my father, who was more easy-going, was sensitive about his epilepsy. They both were. His fits, though he couldn't know it, were spectacular. Sometimes we knew a seizure was imminent. A headache would drag on for days. But equally often he'd collapse in the middle of a sentence or whistling a tune. He'd go for months and then have six in a row. There was no predictable pattern.

I was never aware of being frightened as a child because I saw his fits many times. My mother would take the three heavy cushions from the hide sofa and lay them on the floor. Then, her arms under his and locked on his chest, she'd drag my father's dead weight from wherever he'd fallen over to the cushions. She'd take off his shoes and his tie, open his shirt and loosen his waistband. Then we'd wait. For ten to twenty minutes he would lie there without moving, except for one eyebrow which jigged up and down while his mouth twitched sideways.

48

Suddenly he'd arch his back like a twig in a furnace, scraping his stockinged feet for purchase, then take his head in both hands and try to smash it on the floor, only prevented by the cushions. And he would scream. The screams were the worst part. A priest who happened to be visiting my mother volunteered to stay on one of these occasions, but the screams drove him out.

When he subsided after five minutes, he'd lie with his eyes wide open but unfocused, weeping. My mother would hitch up her skirt and straddle his chest. With her face close to his, she'd say, 'Knobser, Knobser, Knobser, Knobser, Knobser,' in a gentle voice until his eyes focused and he came back to her with a groan of recognition. 'Knobser' was my father's fighting name. 'Young 'un,' he'd say, and she'd go off to make him a cup of tea.

This care, spiced with irritability, wasn't entirely one-way. My father is naturally ebullient but in the 1950s my mother suffered from 'nerves'. This was a mixture of anaemia and depression. The doctor recommended various tonics and she also drank something called Sanatogen – an expensive nerve tonic which, psychologically, seemed to work. Though we children heard a lot about my mother's nerves, we never really saw them in action. If she had bouts of crying, she kept them to herself, or perhaps we simply didn't notice. She lost weight but nothing was allowed to interfere with her work and she regularly sewed till four or five in the morning. The Sanatogen was one of those odd luxuries, like my father's Dettol baths. While my father supported my mother's right to Sanatogen as a necessity, he indulged in his antiseptic baths. Once the tub was full, he'd pour liberally from the bottle, relishing its glottal stop, and watch the water cloud with a great writhing dragon of disinfectant. My mother was always telling

49

him to measure the right amount with the cap of the bottle, but it wasn't his style. He was hardly ever gloomy, but when he was, it always took the same form. My brother and I would be misbehaving noisily. He would have a headache and tell us that when he died we would come and put dandelions on his grave. My mother was more stoical and scorned this self-pity. She had so little of it herself.

She had a natural restraint, unlike my father who, one Sunday night on his way back from chapel, took a short cut over some rough ground and broke his ankle. For a week he suffered the plaster which went up to his knee and terminated in a lump on his instep like someone walking through packed snow. We drew on the cast and autographed it. But finally the itching was too much for him and we got up one morning to find plaster of Paris and remnants of bandage all over the carpet where he had irritably scissored it off at two in the morning. He drank endless cups of tea, too. Chain-drank with three heaped spoons of sugar in each cup and spent longer in the lavatory than anyone else, taking tea, cigarettes and the newspaper with him. He was absorbed in the business of picking horses, from which he did modestly well. But the great dream was winning the football pools. On Saturday evenings, he'd fold open the newspaper at the fixture list and sing the refrain '£75,000' to the signature tune of *Sports Report* (£75,000 was then the top prize dividend paid out by Littlewood's or Vernon's football pool). Anyone who spoke while the results were being read would receive a snarl of disapproval. This was the serious business of becoming rich – a fantasy which involved descriptions of the clinic he would open with the proceeds, the disciples he would train, and the short burst of bad temper or glum despair as he checked his coupon and found he hadn't won. The same meticulous concentration appeared whenever he wrote a letter to the local paper. Everyone had to be totally silent. He didn't find writing easy and the bit he liked best was his signature, an elaborate affair of practised flourishes.

The town I grew up in was a typical, ugly small town in the north of England. My parents still live there and my father loves it and shares its faintly ridiculous pride. There Stephenson built the 'Rocket', the first steam engine. There my father wore the first pair of plus-fours and my mother had the first Eton crop (an accident of her father's home hairdressing). My mother would like to leave, but my father wants to stay where he is known, where he played Blinky Bill in *The Belle of New York* and astounded the audience with the athleticism of his Apache dance. Their children have left instead. It felt an ordinary place, but my father's friend, Billy Llewelyn, could play the saw, grow black carnations, go without sleep for three weeks at a time and expand his chest from thirty-six inches to fifty-two inches in three breaths. The last accomplishment and the saw-playing were a feature of the concert parties. When his chest was fully expanded, he was unable to speak. When he did sleep, he simply went into a trance for five minutes. The night hours he spent gardening by floodlight. I accepted all of this without thinking it in any way unusual, even though my father used to boast about Billy's achievements as if they were a matter for civic pride. Actually, I was more fascinated by his wife who had a TB hip. On my mother's instructions, I always refused any drinks that were offered when we went to visit her.

Anyway, Billy Llewelyn couldn't match my father's curse. The curse was only employed twice – once against the magistrate who fined my father £100 and took away his publican's licence for receiving a stolen lorry load of whisky during the war. My father thought the sentence unjust because he had only agreed to buy a few bottles of bootleg whisky. However, the Canadian who stole the stuff turned up in the middle of the night with a revolver, took all the money my father had, and made him unload the entire cargo. My father was detected when he donated three bottles to the annual police raffle. Typically, because he felt innocent, he thought he *was* innocent. And went on thinking so. Hence the curse on the magistrate from the dock. Results were almost immediate. In a week, his wife was killed in a car crash. The other curse was directed at the committee members of the local Working Men's Club when they banned my father, on the pretext of his epilepsy, but really because he always won at cards and wasn't keen to give people a chance to win their money back. He'd play for a hour or two, then leave. 'Nay, you'll only lose more,' he'd reply when they asked him to stay. Within a fortnight, the committee had reconvened and given my father free life membership. No deaths this time, as I recall, just an unmarried daughter pregnant, a house burned down and an episode of major surgery.

We weren't popular as a family. My mother had social pretensions and candidly looked down on most of our neighbours – feckless social casualties like Mary Haslam who picked coal on the slag heaps and was endlessly pregnant by a series of different partners; like the Races, one of whose children my father caught drinking paraffin. When he told Mrs Race, she clouted the boy across the face and her remark became one of our family jokes: 'I wouldn't care, I wanted it for the lamp.' My father was friendly enough but too obviously confident of his powers: if other parents complained to him about me or my brother, he always took our side and made it clear that he would roll up his sleeves and take on anyone who laid a finger on us. My brother and I behaved with an immune princeliness that was galling. But it was a strange area and we sometimes came unstuck.

I remember one Sunday afternoon when I saw Zebbie the Coalpicker pushing a bicycle up the hill with a sack of coals on the cross-bar. He was supposed to be mad. I shouted at him, 'Ya, Zebbie the Coalpicker', and he chased me with an axe to our back door. Another time, Alan Slab, who later served a life sentence for murder, chased me across the common in the dark for being cheeky. I saved myself by hurling half a brick into the darkness. Luckily, it hit him on the head. Yet, although we condescended to those around, middle-class people weren't enthusiastic about us. I was never invited to parties by the children I admired at school like Kathryn Watson who had a kilt pinned with a great silver safety pin. I decided this was because I never wore a tie and one morning my mother found me trying to tie one of my father's. I didn't explain why and took instead a tartan scarf—to be Rob Roy, I said, but actually to conceal my lack of proper neckwear. Finally, I resolved to have a birthday party like other children, and I nagged my mother until she gave in. Several people turned up, apparently, but only one person agreed to come as I remember it: Alan Chapman, an unposh boy with a big blue scar down his nose. He ate steadily until he had to go. We played no games. He brought no present. We never tried to repeat the occasion.

W. H. Auden once said that he learned to read by taking down the *Encyclopaedia Britannica* from his father's densely stocked shelves. My childhood was less literary. When I was six, my father taught me how to draw profiles. Or rather, faces. It was just that they were all in profile and virtually identical. For the next two or three years, I made elaborate paintings in which figures struck wooden postures and confronted each other in profile.

The effect was Egyptian. I knew then that I was going to be an artist. It never occurred to me that I might become a poet – partly because there were no books in the damp little prefab where we lived. My father read only cowboy books, dogeared and disposable, until my mother jeered at him for wasting his time. After that, he merely sat, smoking Woodbines and idly listening to *Music While You Work* on the radio. This was followed by *Workers' Playtime* – Arthur English and Ken Platt with his catch phrase, 'I won't take my coat off, I'm not stopping.' My mother preferred the daily serial, *Mrs Dale's Diary*, which she mocked a little but rather liked because it was about a doctor's wife. For the same social reasons, she always made us listen to the Queen's Christmas broadcast to the Commonwealth, after we had eaten the annual rabbit pie with suet crust. She was part Mulholland on her mother's side and she knew we had fallen from the middle class or, to be precise, that her mother had married down, even though she loved her father. My own father was similarly descended: he had a cousin Reg who had a *French* wife, Marie. An uncle had been Lord Mayor of York. Other relations had been bishops and aldermen, 'barristers-at-law', but my father was most proud of an uncle who had invented Aero, a kind of chocolate with bubbles of air in it (by accident, as it happened). And he loved to mimic his cousin Marie's accent. The only sign of this lost affluence was a genealogical freak by which my father and his brothers became freemen of the city of York on their twenty-first birthday. The right is hereditary but I've done nothing about it, slightly to my father's chagrin. He sometimes refers wistfully to the possibility.

On the whole, though, he was a happier member of the working class than my mother. Now and again, he could be militant: when Lady Astor gave a speech in which she suggested that ex-servicemen should wear arm bands to warn people that they might have venereal disease, my father shouted her down and called her an ex-chorus girl. And he always seemed to be campaigning vigorously and futilely for some boy or other who had been sent to borstal for a criminal offence. My father didn't believe in prisons. Once when Hugh Dalton, the local MP and a Cabinet Minister, was about to open a factory by snipping the red tape with a pair of ornamental scissors, my father stepped out of the crowd, took the scissors and demanded a house as a disabled ex-serviceman. He got one a week later – the prefab we lived in until I was eleven. The previous house was no good because, with epilepsy, the stairs were a risk and he had already broken most of his ribs. He was always certain he was right and was never awed by the upper classes. Before I was born, my mother lost her three-year-old daughter who had convulsions and died under her hands on the kitchen table. She was exactly three months pregnant at the time and the shock caused her to miscarry. When the doctor wouldn't make the night call, saying it could wait till morning, my father said he would shoot him if my mother died. The doctor came.

My mother cultivated the few cultivated people in town. Every Sunday on our way back from church, we'd call on Mrs Wright, whose son was a Schools Inspector and had been to Cambridge. Mrs Wright was the only person we knew who took the *Observer*. We took the *People* and the *Sunday Post*, neither of them a highbrow paper. Mrs Wright was a widow and deaf and lonely, so my mother's motives were good. All the same, I think my mother was showing me something. She was friendly with Miss Bennison, the retired headmistress, too, and would sometimes return with the strangest books – *The Psychology of Sport and Play* or *School Hygiene for*

Teachers – which were carefully kept for when I was old enough. Some of our relatives were better off than us: they had cars, praised Churchill and voted Conservative, to my father's disgust. There was my cousin Brynley – a dapper little chap, as his name suggests, with his clip-on tartan bow tie, a Jeff Arnold watch, a model aeroplane and other signs of affluence like braces. Half-immersed in a white fur rug, he carelessly consumed Macdonald's chocolate marshmallows and turned over the pages of his *Eagle Annual* in the shadow of the family piano. Bits of Meccano lay around waiting to be pilfered if I'd had the courage. He had all the social skills: I remember watching him tap a mesmeric foot to the tune of 'I Scream, You Scream, We All Scream for Ice Cream'.

His father, my uncle Charlie, organized those concert parties, sold fire extinguishers, swapped cars, was a brilliant sign-writer. His wife, a Rymer, owned part of the dress shop and suffered aristocratically from migraine. In the 1920s, she'd been a great beauty and a sharp dresser. Her house was full of bead curtains and reproduction furniture – a fact which impressed me so much I thought for a long time that Reproduction was a period like Jacobean and Elizabethan. Her eyebrows had been severely plucked in her youth, never to return. When I visited, I carried home great piles of well thumbed women's magazines for my mother. At Christmas I was given one of Brynley's old books with his name crossed out and a torch or a diary thrown in. I think now that they were probably quite generous, but then I took my colour from my proud mother – who retaliated with satire to the implicit condescension she thought she detected.

At home, I mooched about in a pair of basketball boots mended with a bicycle repair kit, eating ketchup on bread, and staring at a wart on my finger the size and texture of a tiny cauliflower. Indoors, my mother baked butterfly cakes, following the instructions in the floury Be-Ro recipe book and dilating sarcastically on 'shop-bought rubbish'. Secretly, we all yearned for the expensive egg-less sort. One day, cousin Brynley's *Eagle Annual* arrived, worn at the corners. I was keener on the pictures than on the prose and therefore skipped most of the moral rearmament propaganda: 'hobbies', like 'pocket money', were things that other kids had, so I was never tempted to make a jet-propelled car with a Sparklets bulb (whatever that was). On the other hand, after a glance at 'Luck of the Legion', I went about for a week with a white handkerchief tucked into the back of my cap, ordering the dog to about-face or wooing it with words of French culled from the strip ('Oo-ee, mon pet it'). The medieval element was a strong influence too: as a result, my mother was cajoled into making me a suede money bag with a draw-string and five polished threepenny bits for sovereigns. I used to sit on the wall, spurring the brick and tossing the purse magnanimously to the dog below. And my father was persuaded to beg a cow's horn from Curly Morland the butcher. We sawed off the point with a neighbour's hacksaw, then forced a hole through with a knitting needle. It hung from my neck secured by a length of dressing-gown cord. Eventually, I managed to coax a strained fart from the horn, but it took hours of practice. I have a memory of my mother slumped, weak with laughter, against our back door.

But mostly the ethos of *Eagle* was too remote from my working-class existence. If it supplied the name for a gang (the Blue Pearl Gang), it left you to invent the enrolment ritual – in our case, peeing into a bottle and letting lighter fuel burn on the palm of your hand. And its suggested 'activities', like rearing silkworms, bore no resemblance to our gang meetings, where we planned raids on greenhouses, smoked cigarette ends picked up in the street or watched Brian Fish eat a live worm. *Eagle* came in useful only once. I got full marks for composition at school by cribbing the life of Albert Schweitzer and claiming I wanted to be a missionary when I grew up.

The pictures were another source of inspiration. Every Saturday found me in the Hippodrome, our nearest cinema, which stood like a red-brick wireless set at the junction of Main Street, Byrely Road and Auckland Terrace. Downstairs, you sat on wooden benches; upstairs, there were seats of dark crimson plush. Everywhere a strong smell of disinfectant and in the concrete corridors grey mops in galvanized buckets. Despite these precautions, I quite often came home with a flea and my mother would take out the streaked bottle of calamine lotion and dab the itchy lumps. Then she would search for the flea, going along the seams of my clothes with her thumbnail until it jumped. 'Don't move.' She'd lick her finger and thumb, pounce calmly, then roll the flea for a few seconds to stun it before she cracked it between her thumb nails. The pictures, though, were worth it. I liked the way the usherette threaded the torn half-tickets on to a long string so they made a branch of monkey-puzzle tree. And I liked the way the satin curtains crinkled out of sight. Dim scratchy advertisements for Ernie Calvert's Watch Repairs and Gus Bentley's Bike Shop appeared on the screen. Gus, who in real life had black finger-ends cross-hatched like a file and no nails to speak of, smiled benignly out from the rain storm, his hair carefully combed, hands hidden under the counter. I sat right at the front, my head tilted back as if for a nose-bleed, the stick of my sherbert lolly angled like a thermometer, in a quiet fever of excitement.

The first film I saw was *The Great Caruso*, starring Mario

Lanza. My mother was with me, so we sat upstairs. My father never went to the cinema because the technicolour was bad for his epilepsy. I remember my mother cried towards the end, opening her handbag to take out an embroidered handkerchief so I caught a whiff of 'Evening in Paris', whose blue bottle stood on her dressing table at home, its silver trademark of the Eiffel Tower reflected in triplicate. After that, I usually went on my own, walking home in the dark up the middle of the street. I should have gone to the children's matinée but the serial, *Spider Man*, was too frightening. Then I could walk home in daylight, but at bedtime I still searched my room for the murderer, who wore a black leather built-up surgical boot that swung and lurched down thick-pile carpets towards his victims. The camera shrewdly concealed all other details.

Another icon of terror was Jack Palance in *Apache*. This film must have been given an 'A' certificate by the censors but adults were easily persuaded to 'take us in, please, mister.' A locomotive complete with its iron curtsey of cowcatcher slithers to a halt, bringing Jack Palance, the Apache chief's son, home from schooling back East. Wearing a tidy black suit, Palance throws his carpetbag negligently into the back of Jeff Chandler's buggy which is to take him to the reservation. On the way, in answer to some question about his education, Palance replies by sweeping off his broad-brimmed black hat. His shoulder-length jet-black hair falls dramatically and we see his face clearly for the first time – high-cheek-boned, eyes like slits of molten anthracite. For weeks he was the trouble of my dreams and it took real courage to go to see him in *Attila the Hun*.

I first fell in love at the cinema – with Bella Darvi, a Czech film star who only made two films, *Hell and High Water* with Richard Widmark and *The Egyptian* with

Edmond Purdom. To see *The Egyptian*, I had to walk to the other end of town, to the Essoldo. I took good care to spruce myself up, particularly my hair. (There was nothing I could do about my khaki shorts except tighten the wizened Dan Dare belt that Brynley had passed on.) My hair was curly but I wanted a single, pure wave at the front like a bulldozer. I tried water and one of my mother's Marcel wave grips, a bulldog grip with extra teeth, curved like a miniature coathanger. In the end, though, I had to use my father's Brylcreem. I applied a couple of generous handfuls and styled away until my quiff was cast in bronze. Throughout *The Egyptian* Brylcreem trickled down my brow and stung my eyes. Bella Darvi wore a cobra hat and eyeliner like a tennis racket whose handle stretched to her ears. But it was her last film and after that I had to make do with Jean Simmons in *Desirée*.

At the same time, I had begun to read books. Aged nine, I joined the library and was introduced by a boy called Sid Staveley to the photographs in Lord Russell of Liverpool's *The Scourge of the Swastika*, a bulging book bound in jaundiced polythene which was kept in the adult section. Its atrocities escaped me completely. And the moral polemic. I remember still, though, a photograph of nude, overweight women being made to run through a wet courtyard. One, nearest the camera, was blurred. I remember being unable to connect those grainy breasts and pubic hair with anything in my own life – flesh, for instance – but the image gave me a mysterious frisson which I mistakenly took for sex. The books I actually borrowed from the library – the bad-tempered bump of the date stamp dying in my ears – were adventure stories. I read two a day for two years and forgot them.

The most important book I possessed was not, strictly speaking, a book at all. On the back of the *Topper*, a comic I read at the time, was a serial of Robert Louis Stevenson's

Kidnapped, told almost entirely in pictures. Beneath each frame there was a scrap of token text which I suppose I must have read. I saved up these back pages until I had a complete set and my mother sewed them together on her treddle-operated Singer machine. This 'book' was where I spent most of my childhood. Thirty years later, I can still recall particular images – Alan Breck's silver button set on a wooden cross and placed as a sign in the window of a but and ben; redcoats prodding the heather with their bayonets while Breck and David Balfour sweltered out the day on the top of a huge granite boulder; Breck lowering his belt so that Balfour could scramble up; a chieftain's hide-out somehow built using the trees. To this day I have never read Stevenson's text.

When I was eleven, I won a scholarship to a local public school where Robin, another rich cousin, a Mulholland, was already a pupil. His father, my uncle John, had made his money by selling birds' eggs. The scholarship paid my tuition fees and half my board. The remainder was paid for partly by the county education authority, partly by my mother's long stints at the sewing machine. The RAF Benevolent Fund made an initial contribution towards my clothes, and Mr Grice, their representative, would come round after work and help my mother fill in the forms. My father's way of showing his gratitude was to collect money for the Fund on Wings Day which commemorates the Battle of Britain. He was busy trying to break all records in the charity business. No one was allowed to pass without a contribution: he knew everyone and covered the clubs, the pubs, the chip shops, the football ground. Each day he'd return with ten cans heavy with coins, five to a hand, the strings cutting his fingers. He broke all records, but it was my mother who filled in the forms.

I was bought a large trunk and Uncle Charlie came round one Saturday morning and sign-wrote my name on both ends, with my house number. On my last afternoon at home, surrounded by grey shirts and socks, I looked from the window and saw Bobby Bowen in his best suit with the extra wide trousers walking quickly down the hill, whistling beautifully as he always did, with lots of grace notes. And I remembered how my father had once interfered when Bobby's wife Ena had lost her temper with one of her sons. The boy was cowering outside. She stood, fat, filling the doorway, holding a full-size plastic rifle, shouting, 'In. In. *In*.' Finally, the boy tried to squirm past her like a silverfish but she had him by the hair and was breaking the rifle over his head and shoulders when my father stopped her. He was, as he could be, abusive: he called her a 'fat sadist'. It was the first time I had come across the word. He came back and used another word I knew of course but had never heard my father, or any adult, say before. My mother dashed in from the kitchen, 'Norman, there's *no* excuse for *that*.' It was enough. We got on with our game of chess and, as usual, I exploded with anger when he cheated. 'Are you sure you want to move your queen there?' I'd say. 'When you take your finger off, you can't change it, you know. All right, you've taken your finger off. Are you sure? This is your last chance. OK?' But it wasn't OK and when I reached for my bishop, he'd wave his arms over the board like a referee who's just counted somebody out – and change his move.

I thought that by going away to school I would be leaving nothing behind. Bobby would still whistle in his brown double-breasted suit. My Rudd Cup football medal would nestle in its cotton wool till I got back in the holidays. In fact, I was leaving my father behind. I was completely proud of him and he was proud of me. He was the only father who ever came to our primary school football matches. He would race up and down the touchline, shouting advice and encouragement. At half-time, he'd come on to the pitch and give the whole team extra-strong mints, rearrange the tactics, change our positions, tell us we were playing downhill in the second half, tell us that a six-goal deficit was nothing. Mr Newby, the teacher nominally in charge, would suck a mint and listen like the rest of us. We won every game. He willed us to do it.

At my boarding school, I learned to be ashamed of him. It was a complicated process. I was very much his son and it was six or seven weeks before I learned that the self-confidence he'd given me, genetically and by example, to other people was mere boasting. Modesty wasn't something he'd taught me. I knew when I had played the best game on the rugby field. I remembered my father's story of how he'd played in a game 'against the pick, the *pick*, of Catterick Camp' and won it single-handed by tackling again and again a big winger from the Scots Guards. I had been brought up to be a hero. Gradually, I was made to feel unpopular and I applied these new standards to him. In the first few days, too, I was made to realize my relative poverty. My father had taught me to do a proper somersault. I would bounce on a bed till I was high enough, then I'd do the turn, backwards and forwards. I was showing this off in my first week – wishing I could walk on my hands too, like my father – when I broke the bed's cast-iron frame. The school bursar, to whom I had to report the damage, was stern but not unkind. 'You must realize, Raine 3,' he said, 'that you are different from the other boys. Your parents can't afford to pay for a new bed. The school won't charge you this time, but you must cut your coat according to your cloth.' I broke no more beds and when

Humphreys, whose father was a market gardener, asked me what my father did, I said he was a football manager. I told Manders he was a brain surgeon.

I was at school for seven years. It wasn't until my second year that I told anything like the truth about my father. I had been taken out to lunch by Wakefield's grandparents one Sunday. 'What does your father do?' the old man asked, a trickle of fat in the cleft of his chin. 'He's war disabled,' I replied. I couldn't lie to an adult. 'So you're on a scholarship, then?' 'Yes,' I said. It wasn't so bad, after all.

Yet I must have conveyed some uneasiness to my parents. Perhaps my father couldn't be bothered, perhaps he was worried about his unpredictable epilepsy (I was), but he never came to see the school. My mother would visit on Speech Day and Sports Day, wearing a Jaeger-style home-made camel coat and a pillbox hat, or her green velvet coat that made her look, I thought, like the Queen. If she was uneasy, she disguised it well. I was sixteen before I took any of my school friends home. They adored my father. He told them dirty jokes, irrepressible as ever.

And I felt rich again.

Not even kissed by self-contempt.

Part III

Poor

Drinking-water was brought, in two cracked Worcester cups and three cocoanut shells on a silver salver.
Richard Hughes, *A High Wind in Jamaica*

A Walk in the Country

Letè vedrai, ma fuor di questa fossa,
   là dove vanno l' anime a lavarsi . . .
                                    Dante, *Inferno* XIV

The muddy lane
is its own
travel document,

obliterate
with a variety
of stamps

which allow us
this journey beyond
the sewage farm

like a tape-recorder,
whose black spools
turn night and day

as excrement
patiently eavesdrops
on peace.

It is a machine
that remembers
the sounds of nothing . . .

They are burning
the stubble
in the fields ahead,

67

which is why
the graveyard seems
ringed with fire

and somehow forbidden.
Is it fear
halting my child

so that her thumb,
withdrawn for a second,
smokes in the air?

Or fascination
like her father's?
I bend and watch

the stalks melt
when I purse my lips
for a morbid kiss

and blow a bright,
whispering ulcer
in the blackened straw.

One swallow
sways on a wire
like a grain

of whiskered barley,
saved from the flames.
Do not be afraid:

there are men
on the roof of the church,
playing patience,

tile after tile,
and here is a man
gardening a grave

methodically,
lost in the rituals
of growth.

His jacket is folded,
lining-side out,
and laid on a headstone

as he tends
to his fainted plants,
carefully unwrapping

the dark, moist newsprint.
Without thinking,
I roll away a stone

with my foot
and find this toad
with acorn eyes

and a brown body
delicate as a drop
of dusty water

yet still intact
and hardly surprised
by resurrection.

The Widower

His wet waders
dipped in lacquer
by the light,

the lobsterman
puts out to sea
against the tide

that tilts his boat.
From where we stand,
up on the dunes,

his wicker pots
have dwindled already
to balls of twine,

but for five minutes,
saluting the sun
out of our eyes,

we watch him knit
with clumsy oars,
while the waves

unravel their length,
this way, that way,
on the beach below . . .

Have we come here
to forget
her funeral,

or have we come
to hold her memory
intact again?

Seeing jelly fish
like wilted Dali watches
all along the shore,

who can tell
what dispensations
are possible in time?

She might still be here,
I sometimes feel,
walking slowly

back to the cottage:
there are ghosts
in the hedge

where sheep press through.
I pat the solid sand
until it liquefies

beneath my foot,
reminding me
of how the world

was turned to water
by the candle flame
beside her coffin,

how a crucifix
shuddered
and stonework drowned

as the priest looked on
with midnight hands
at ten in the morning.

What is real?
The congregation slipping
their spectacles on

to sing the hymn?
The straining bearers
like a string quartet,

taking the burden up
in unison, at a nod
from their leader?

Those whitened fingertips?
The widower rambles,
unburying shells

with his alpenstock.
Specs on his forehead,
he brings each one

close to his better eye,
before discarding
nearly everything.

Somewhere in my head
she is pushing aside
her breakfast tray.

I can see her smile,
a timeless crumb
of yolk

precarious
in the hairs
beside her mouth.

Plain Song

There was the chiropodist,
whose wife had a tapeworm
or a fallopian cyst,
and there was my father

reading his tea-leaves.
I was hidden behind the sofa
and could only see a turn-up
and one ox-blood Saxone loafer:

I'd taken all my clothes off
for the lavatory, hours before,
and now Mr Campbell had come.
My mother shut the kitchen door,

firmly, like a good Catholic,
snubbing the two Spiritualists.
I imagined the best china
in my father's massive fists:

a woman in hoops and crinoline,
the dainty rustic handle,
the Typhoo hieroglyphics,
the fate of Mrs Campbell

whom mother felt so sorry for.
My father went into control
and I listened, out of sight,
to the jumbled rigmarole:

someone was passing over
to another world of love.
Why do I only now discover
the woman's thin voice

saying she will be missed,
my father's eyes rolled back
and Mr Campbell's unhappy mouth,
open like a bad ventriloquist?

Again

If he utters the sound for pain,
the one with cardboard clothes

will punish his pillows
and let him listen to the heart

she wears outside on a safety pin,
the better to show her love

whenever she holds his hand.
Unless the foreigners bring flowers,

she is deaf twice a day
and hard to disturb,

being busy with homework –
sandwiches she reads just once

and then recites from memory.
His breath is a bluebottle,

trapped alive inside his chest,
and half of his face doesn't exist,

so he can never contrive
the shape of pleasure

he's seen the foreigners make
if they manage to say *Gor-don*,

his appallingly difficult name,
which always sounds like a question.

Otherwise, meaning eludes them:
unlike the studious, silent one,

they are often disfigured by sounds,
sounds with a terrible taste

to be swiftly spat out.
He has deduced that objects

need love because they are lonely.
Everything touches something else.

Being is lost if the law is broken.
Example: the silverglass rod

which belonged to the bending bowl
which belongs to the table

which belongs to the floorboards.
His servant borrowed the rod

for its story, read, then tried
to shake it from her fingers,

where, according to the law, it clung
until she gave it to his mouth,

choosing the absent side
where contact was lost. He heard

the cry of its dissolution, saw
the blood run away from itself

on the floorboards below.
Example: the infatuated mug

that stuck to his blotchy hand
when he started with homework.

The table refused to take it
till someone unclenched his grip.

Example: he belongs to his bed.
Where would he be without it?

Answer: far away from his flesh
which has been tricked into sleep

without his permission
by these garments of numbness.

Bound by anaesthetic shoes,
he moves without moving,

cold in the invisible water,
along the looms of perception,

with a sense of loss in his hand
and crying for the cloth of comfort

with which he could banish the world.
Now the choirs of nausea sing . . .

He wakes to a different prison bed,
the captive now of foreigners,

finding his body at last returned.
From a hook on the door,

the garments hang deformed
but every day they must be worn.

The foreigners force them on
and torture his mouth with the bones

which painfully insist
on the shape of pleasure.

As if from a forgotten mirror,
a face he knows has come today

with undeniable arms
to dance him out into space,

out and down to another room.
It is his replica, his youth,

from somewhere before before,
who puts him helpless in this chair.

Baize Doors

She had forgotten the bellows again
and the family was due back from church.
Her mind was on the gardener's boy,

who'd left her in the lurch
the Friday before: without his reference,
leaving only a collar stud behind

at the back of a paper-lined drawer,
and that drawn length of linen blind
which curtsied gently in her hand

then vanished when she let it go.
She knew that she must be alive
by her breath on the window

when she deliberately adjusted
an hairpin, before going downstairs . . .
The bellows were kept in the kitchen

beyond the bottle-green baize
where the floral carpet stopped
and the stone steps started.

No one had ever fallen before.
The under-cook was broken-hearted
about the blood and slipped

a *Reynold's News* between her floor
and the opened skull. Morgan, the valet,
was dispatched for the doctor,

who turned the face to find
a phrenologist's head: the stop press
transferred backwards on the brain.

The gardener's boy was on her mind.
A pair of bellows prayed in the hearth.
The kitchen fire fell to its death.

The Season in Scarborough 1923

for Martin Amis

Inches below
her sagging mattress,
the suitcase

lay forgotten,
light as an egg
blown by a brother . . .

Six months served
among the rich,
so many years ago:

the silver blister
on the kedgeree
for breakfast,

vaccinated spoons,
the bidet
and its replica,

the avocado
(halved, then served
with *vinaigrette*)

were themes
for letters home
on headed sheets.

No mention
of irate saucepans
letting off steam,

the soapy ghost
of caviar
in the washing up . . .

Plus-fours, plaids,
Turkish cigarettes
made home absurd –

a line of cottages
with vulgar wigs
in wire hairnets.

She felt herself
a debutante,
dropping curtsies

to the brogues
put out at night
for polishing

and she loved
her linen tiara
pinned in place.

On odd days off,
she rode the funicular
up and down

the South Cliff,
two French phrases
aromatic

in her mouth:
the far-away feel
of *Es-tu seule*? –

like the thought
of someone
touching her breasts . . .

On the train
to literary London,
my season ticket

about to expire,
I think of her
the day she packed,

suddenly homesick
for the real . . .
Why is it

sandy ulcers
on some suburban,
sodden golfcourse

can dazzle me,
as if I were
her dusty suitcase,

dreaming cardboard,
startled open
by the plosive locks?

Circus

These circus people
wean their children late:
double-jointed steps

unfold from a caravan
and a mother sits,
staring at her thoughts,

while men arrange
the masts and get
the big top under sail –

her baby press-stud close.
Tethered by a foot,
their sole giraffe

manipulates its jib
like an Anglepoise,
awkwardly precise.

The circus strong man
in his off-the-shoulder
Amazonian leotard

will reveal one pap
and twitch directories
in half this afternoon

like slightly obdurate
entrance tickets,
but now he plays

his careful breath
to part two clinging
pages of (can it be?)

Copperfield in paperback.
My daughter tells me
she has seen a man

behind a trailer
with seven tangerines
he shares out equally

between both hands . . .
Listening to the tick
of unseen hammers

in the tented dark,
I can just make out
the faintly luminous

set of drums –
a great alarm clock,
fast asleep.

For the circus
is dreaming its dream,
in which there are

no bull terriers
in tartan trousers
pushing about prams,

no usherette
by Salvador Dali
with a drawer in her midriff

full of ice cream,
no one mincing the length
of an impossible wire,

no sequinned, suddenly
foetal acrobats,
no one lurching

like Richard the Third
in the safety net,
no scorpion contortionist,

heels over head . . .
Nothing of this, only
a ring of porridge oats,

one tufted coconut
like the last
of the Mohicans,

a tin of French chalk
and a trainer's whip
frayed at the end.

Only a woman at sea,
nursing her need
to be normal,

who wills the circus
to melt in the sun
like a dirty iceberg.

The Sylko Bandit

Sir Walter Raleigh, when they arrested him, had half a
million francs on his back, including a pair of fancy stays.

James Joyce, *Ulysses*

Something apt to garden,
he does plant those naked boys,
the finest of Holland,
along the length of windowe box.

Were it not for the Buddha,
the whiche he hath acquired
from out of Angkor Wat,
stone melted lobes intact,

he does much resemble a poet,
one that ekes out guilders
in payment for his rented room
hard by the station,

whose terminus of zips
provokes his smile,
for that it semes
an ironie writ large . . .

Yet consider him now,
preparing state cocaine
for guestes, above ten lines,
from the gouverment kiosk:

he is the vnexpected thyng,
who values not those laws
long passed enforcing playnesse,
being a smuggler of velvets,

a connoisseur of cloths,
and that despite a good degree,
an Oxford first in drugs,
both divisions of the tripos.

Sick affrayd of sumptuary police,
we do fear his flamboyaunce
and that fearless way he hath
of strolling to the windowe,

the better there to criticize
some new edition of sylks,
scanning thro them like a scholar.
Small wonder we sweat.

We are vnprepared
for all his compromising giftes
that make us poor,
being ready for something els:

politics, dissent, our bravery.
We did use to practise speeches.
But no man could predict
thys educated laughter,

the grounding in Freud,
learned journals, broken spines,
and a time when cloths
would be cause of betrayal.

He much resembles a psycholeech
in that he vnderstandes
the threat that we fele
from fire appliances

whiche do press them into corners,
darkly, like spies, on each flight
of the stairs. He knoweth our fear
whiche is affrayd of the concierge,

her talkative needles,
their whispered mors code.
We love him. We hate him.
He is too rich to trust.

No matter if we will or no,
the telephone is in our hand,
waking the 'ragge-trade',
asleep in playn-clothes.

Taffeta, grosgraine, bullion,
velvet, satin and chiffon,
samite, sylk and chenille:
it is time at last

to practise betrayal,
like one that recites
from a favourite poem,
slowly, with love,

yet heareth only thys,
the squash court in the heart,
and reads a verdict
in the railway lines . . .

twenty year with temperatures.

A Hungry Fighter

It is well known that I am a prize fighter by profession
. . . I am now writing a New Canto of Don Juan . . .
                              John Clare to Eliza Phillips (1841)

The headguard's padded pith
protects my father's face.
Juice erupts in tiny sacs
like smallpox through the vaseline.

He steams in the morning cold,
trailing clouds of glory
through the hard acoustic gym,
that spring of 1932.

High-handed, hinges of hair
in his streaming armpits,
he drubs this leather fig –
attentive to its anapaests

until the one includes the many.
A single giant salami
forms part of his diet;
the twelve-ounce gloves

are raw sienna curves
like parrot tongues,
bluntly repeating
again and again

a phrase book of grunts.
His mind translates
the tick of skipping ropes
until the big time fills his head.

He hears a Pentecostal wind.
Scales flinch under his feet:
this featherweight of whiteness
is all he has for sale.

After the southpaw Johnny Magorie,
a title fight with Micky McGuire:
they duck into the ring,
black bottom briefly

in the fuming trays of rosin,
then bumps-a-daisy, glove
on glove. The referee
patrols the bandaged ropes,

dapper in his black bow tie.
A cut begins to irrigate
above the champion's eye.
My father slips a lead

and flicks the cut,
his fluent fists
clenched question marks
to which there is no answer.

McGuire takes a count of six
then, breaking from a clinch,
he crosses with a right
that finds the throat.

Helpless as a naked girl,
my father covers up
then crawls like a baby
baring his gumshield.

His second threw the towel in –
a thick Turkish towel
like fleecy tripe,
left behind in the Albert Hall.

The gym is rubble now,
a bathos of bricks
by the railway line,
Russian salad out in the rain.

I will inherit his vest,
its English rose, one petal
darned, his boxing licence
with the rusty staples,

the silver-plated cup
presented by von Ribbentrop
which stands on the sideboard,
confidently arms akimbo

but worn away by Duraglit.
Touching their terror,
I gaze at them now,
longer than someone in love.

The Gift

Had a secret hinge, was scented
with sandalwood from Lebanon,
was 'a gift for a wedding',
was an ordinary gift
yet contained all our life.

Intricate with images,
it cried *behold*:
behold this thaw of goats
on the Caucasus, behold
the carpetbagger bees

caught up in their gold rush,
the ejaculate salmon
and the heliograph sea.
The gift held everything
we once had owned:

Kiev, her winter windows
like a photographic album
with simple mounts of snow,
a curtain call of flowers
for sale at every corner,

a grand piano which rested
its head in its hand,
listening to Mozart
when lamps were lit
and the samovar brought.

And other memories
like pain still sulking
somewhere in a finger joint:
the German shower set
curled in the bath

like a flugelhorn,
our pencilled heights
on the nursery door,
a shoal of two-inch nails
that shone in the cellar.

The gift was everything
and everything in gold.
But we showed the box,
its clever carvings,
and lifted the lid on emptiness.

A gift for a wedding,
a wedding close to the frontier,
our guide explained,
pausing to spit,
when the soldiers pressed.

Yes, they said, we understand.
This watch is gold?
Later you claim this watch
on your way from the wedding.
Now, where are your papers?

The papers we carried
were the old big banknotes
that folded in four.
My father's wallet had a thong
and opened like a triptych

from Kiev to Khotin,
until we took that train
with all its windows broken
which brought us to Cracow.
Where my father shaved

in a bowl of hot water
while mother recited *Onegin*,
where we sat down at table
to the gifts of the gift:
soup and sausage and bread.

The Man Who Invented Pain

He lifted the wicker lid
and pigeons poured
past his hands,

a ravel of light
like oxygen
escaping underwater.

Loss of privileges
in peacetime; in war,
a capital offence.

He offered no defence,
simply composed
a non-existent life

in letters home,
enough for a year,
to be posted in order,

of which the last began:
Dear Mother, Dear Dad,
Thanks for yours.

Today, a Tuesday,
we shot a man
at 0800 hours.

Try to imagine,
if you can,
the subdued feel

of a Sunday morning
and the quiet clash
of a dixie lid,

lifting and lapsing
like a censer
at mass.

Imagine held hats,
blown about hair
and the firing squad

down on one knee,
close enough to see
his Adam's apple

genuflect
just once
before they fired.

And then imagine
the rest of the day:
the decent interval

before the men
began to form a queue
with mess tins,

the way in which
the day remained
a Sunday until dark.

Things were touched
with reverence.
Even the sergeant,

feeling for fags
in his battle dress,
patted his pockets

uncertainly,
in turn, and again,
as if he'd forgotten

the sign of the cross,
and the captain
on a canvas stool

sat like a priest,
with praying eyes
and inclined head,

while his batman cut
and curls fell
all over his surplice.

Imagine the sun
waking the flies
to a confessional buzz

in the camp latrines,
and each latrine
a taut box kite

waiting for wind
on the kind of day
a man might read

the Sunday paper
by his pigeon cree,
or nervously

walk out to bat
and notice the green
on a fielder's knee.

Purge

His name is called terror
and always he begins like this:
the boxing match is killed,
leave to make jokes is cancelled.
Instead the radio sings Sibelius
and Mozart's Concerto for Horn

and we know again the fear of classical
music.

I have been by the garden
since dawn, with a silver fork
(a wedding gift from formerly
when our love was little in years).
I have buried the past,
making my possessions shy

and now I have a headache in my heart.

My eight-day Swiss chronometer
is criminal against the State:
she does not tell the time
correct for salting meat.
The Nikon hurts my conscience too:
her tale-tell scrolls

belong to underground with Johnnie Walker.

They are only in love
with chapped hand and chopstick.
Their heart keeps indoors,
unhappy with agoraphobia,
if a book is found abroad.
They are a poorest people

which makes a crime of my English
                                    grammar.

Bury H. G. Wells and Arnold Bennett,
Forsyte Saga and forget.
Illegible and poised to dive,
I squat in these veranda steps
like Patience on the Monument.
I am almost nearly prepared

for I have tidied all it up, my life.

There on the stream their junk
is perched, a butterfly
that feeds the flowers.
Is it called a cabbage white?
And I feel hunger also too.
I take off this banana's coat

and proffer pieces to my wife which
                                    shakes its head.

It is weeping tears.
In the smallest time now,
I will discover guilt,
caught with possession
of pianist hands.
Who cannot be buried.

Who mean not Mozart but laxative and
letting blood.

The Grey Boy

The captain takes a swig
at scratched binoculars,
while we light the fires
with Act One of *Lear*.

There is no music now,
only food in the branches
and sometimes a sing-song
of corpses across the river,

rising like dough.
Hush. Somewhere out of sight,
but close, close, food talks
to the captain, describing itself:

the soil on its beak,
its paranoid eye.
He believes the inedible claws
as once he believed in God,

as children now believe
in the grey boy. Is it
a wren like a pinch of snuff?
Another swig: eloquent saliva,

the gift of tongues.
He reads the livid prolapse
on a silver birch. Gone.
The magnifying glass

concentrates on a single word
until it bursts into flames
and talks to us. Now.
Speaking of heat. Asking for twigs.

We are not afraid of the sunset.
We are used to the sunset
burning its medicines.
When it is over, we sleep,

waiting for food to break its silence.
The mind is a museum
to be looted at night:
'A piece of toilet soap,

still wet, Imperial Leather,
the pale underbelly
reminiscent of plaice.'
'A cheese in protective bandages.'

These things are old,
old as the *Life of Johnson*
and most of Shakespeare.
Many pages old, including the index.

And still they nourish
when we sleep in the nests,
during the night
when the grey boy comes

to pinch the children
and pull out their hair.
Even the captain's holster
cannot keep him away,

because he doesn't exist.
I can almost describe him:
imagine a milkman, imagine
a milkman collecting a ghost.

The First Lesson

I returned. But the strong
had gone from my fingers
and the key would not turn.

A sea urchin was somehow
under my tongue. And I wept
for the glistening frenum

and the pleasure of words.
For the silence had fallen
and was falling still.

Where the threshold was worn
like a much sharpened knife,
I waited to enter.

Thinking, thinking on this:
how the heir to a throne
had queued for a razor blade

and a Cadbury's Flake,
and counted his change,
who once owned the forest,

the deep, wet field,
the grinder of knives
and his trickle of sparks.

Who sleeps in a dirty vest,
remembering regiments
and all the butterflies

that settled on epaulettes,
their catkins of gold,
when the day reached an end.